THE LANGUAGE OF WATER AND GRASS

THE LANGUAGE OF WATER AND GRASS

Collected Poems

Judson D. McGehee

GLEN
LYON
PRESS

Glen Lyon Press, LLC
Flagstaff, Arizona
Visit our website at **www.glenlyonpress.com**

THE LANGUAGE OF WATER AND GRASS

Front Cover Photograph: Marshall Lake - Tracy Wesolek / Dreamstime.com

ISBN: 978-1-942461-03-6
Library of Congress Control Number: 2023940344

ACKNOWLEDGEMENTS

Grateful acknowledgment is made to the editors of those publications where the below poems first appeared:

Reed: "Lines at a Leprosarium" (May 1954)

Generation: "Origins", "War and the Ueno Zoo: to the Tiger" (Vol 7, No. 1, 1955)

Poems Southwest: "House Mouse", "Sunset Crater", "The Vultures of Walnut Canyon" (1968)

Quetzal: "On the Trail to Rainbow Bridge" (Vol. I, No. 3, Summer 1971)

Quetzal: "West Clear Creek", "Hart Prairie Herder" (Vol. II, No. 3, Summer 1972)

Crescendo: A Growing Anthology: "Gone", "The Long Rain" (February 1974)

Adventures in Sounds and Similes: "Red Tail Hawk" (1974)

A special thank you to the late Paul A. Sweitzer of the *Arizona Daily Sun* for supporting the weekly column, *Northland Nature*, which included the following poems:

"Ponderosa" – as "Ponderosa, a Winter Poem" (February 17, 1978)

"West Clear Creek" (September 30, 1979)

"Pond Water: The Microscope" (November 4, 1979)

"East Pocket, West Wall, Oak Creek Canyon" (December 16, 1979)

"Sparrow Hawk" (January 27, 1980)

"Hart Prairie Herder" (March 9, 1980)

"Beaver Dam on West Fork" (March 30, 1980)

"On the Trail to Rainbow Bridge" (April 13, 1980)

"Gone" (May 11, 1980)

"Sunset Crater" (May 25, 1980)

"Vultures of Walnut Canyon" (June 1, 1980)

"House Mouse" (June 22, 1980)

"The Swimmer" (September 7, 1980)
 "Encounter" (October 5, 1980)
"End of August" (October 12, 1980)
"Deadman's Wash" (November 2, 1980)
"The Long Rain" (November 16, 1980)
"Grand Canyon" (December 14, 1980)
"Old House, Old Yard" (January 11, 1981)
"Lindbergh Spring" (February 8, 1981)
"Antelope Wash" (April 5, 1981)
"Spring Safari" – as "Red Rock Safari" (April 19, 1981)
"In the Penultimate Dark" (October 11, 1981)
"Antelope Wash" (February 14, 1982) – revised
"Spring Safari" (February 21, 1982) – revision of "Red
    Rock Safari"
"Summer Monsoon" (August 22, 1982)
"Lindisfarne" (October 24, 1982)
"All Music Haunts Me" (October 31, 1982)
"Dry Lake Hills" (September 5, 1982)
"Steps, Not to be Taken" (December 19, 1982)
"Dry Lake Elegy" (January 20, 1985) – revision of "Dry
    Lake Hills"
"Monsoon Summer" (March 23, 1986) – revision of
    "Summer Monsoon"
"Journey to the Interior" (April 13, 1986)
"Spring Safari" (September 7, 1986) – reprint from
    February 21, 1982
"Norfolk Island Pine" (September 21, 1986)
"Meditations on the Hunter's Moon" (October 19, 1986)
"The Tao of the Hunt" (December 14, 1986)
"This Slant of Light" (January 16, 1987)
"Wet Beaver Creek" (February 6, 1987)
"Sunset Crater" (March 6, 1987) – reprint from
    May 25, 1980
"The Voices of Marshall Lake" (April 17, 1987)

As long as I live, I'll hear waterfalls and birds
and winds sing. I'll interpret the rocks, learn the
language of flood, storm, and the avalanche. I'll
acquaint myself with the glaciers and wild
gardens, and get as near the heart of the world
as I can.

— John Muir

CONTENTS

FOREWORD:
ON THE POETRY OF NATURE

THE POETRY of nature is the poetry of the full or twofold consciousness. It reaffirms the seamless unity that exists between ourselves and the natural world and which we feel when, passing through the barrier of loneliness, our sense of individual isolation bursts into the "all feeling" of identity with the universe.

If we feel alienated from nature, it is not because we have developed an individualized consciousness, but because we have lost the full consciousness we had before we became trapped in the artifice of a linear, conceptual, and categorizing language—a language that often falsifies experience. In learning to deal with nature intellectually, we have withdrawn from the external world of which we are a part.

Being alive, nature is more a process than a thing, and the "things" in it are part of the process and mutually dependent. Thoreau wrote, "The most sweet and tender, the most innocent and encouraging society may be found in any natural object." This is not just Thoreau's way of saying that every natural object symbolizes something to the person who experiences it. The relationship goes deeper. Robert Grave echoed Thoreau when he wrote, "Among trees, you are usually alone, but seldom lonely; they are companionable presences . . ."

I have always been curious about man's relationship with nature and about the origins of those feelings I have experienced in nature. In what sense is a stone conscious, and how do I become aware of the consciousness of a stone? How do I know there is "moonlight inside the stone?" First we must realize that just because an object is non-human does not mean that it is inhuman or anti-human. Its purposes, whatever they are, do not deny our purposes. The stone may not be hostile or moral or friendly or indifferent. But to say what it is not is not to say what it is.

It may be that, for the poet, the mystery of life is not a problem to be solved but a reality to be experienced. To assume that what is not conscious is unconscious is to fall into the language trap—the trap of a language that offers only mutually exclusive alternatives. Perhaps we should only ask, what do we feel the stone is; what do we feel the stone feels? The emotions are as sure a guide to truth as reason.

Only a state of full consciousness, of wordless and profound awareness, allows us to know what nature is like from the inside. Such total awareness may grant to us that high degree of sensitivity to the seamless unity of nature that we lost when we evolved systems of symbolic thought. We must see through and beyond words to the "stillness in the tops of the pines." Conscious efforts to analyze and understand nature only strengthen the dividing mode of consciousness since we always think with words, and words are ideas, not natural objects.

The poet speaks, not of ideas about things, but of the things themselves. The poetry of nature can only be understood through the language of poetry, which is the only language which uses words to go beyond words. Only by denying the literal truth of words can the poet express the inexpressible. The poem's content cannot be paraphrased, translated, or reduced to prose. The images are felt in their singularity and isolation. Moonlight joins them.

It seems, then, that awareness is all, and if my mind does not flow out to nature, nature won't come in to it. I must "enter the poem" but "leave the room" of my self-considering ego. The sense of full consciousness is always mutual and always returned. When I walk alone, or with a sympathetic companion with whom I share my awareness of the non-human that surrounds us and of which we both are a part, I walk through the paradise gardens. The stones come alive, and the trees speak to me.

1 / ON THE TRAIL TO RAINBOW BRIDGE

STRAWBERRY CRATER

The going and coming was enough
in a day of silence;
the slate gray cinders soft
as tropical sand
and all the grasses gold—
pale gold of winter saltbush;
all tones of gray.

It seemed an old and moody dominance,
impressionist's economy of color
begrudging green of adolescent piñons,
Mormon tea.

A scene so large absorbs
shadows below the lava dike,
the smudge-blue of early March,
shallows of wet snow shining,
and the melt that mists the distance
or still stands wintering the northern slopes.

The wind is absent;
we stand in awakening silence,
silence like absence
while the sun
the sun burns gray.

EAST POCKET, WEST WALL,
OAK CREEK CANYON

Daybreak brings fire forth
like wry foxes,
little foxes with black wet feet
and burnished brushes.

It is sun on the presence
of the time telling cliff
whose sandstone sings of home,
of the press of water and the pulse of wind.

Face to the wall
at each decisive turn,
I force the switchbacks
of the plunging ridge
preoccupied with
the great red hurt of my lungs,
the foot turning talus,
and the problem it poses
of the fall.

I who might, conversely, slip
come squealing down
through scrub oak and the unfelt crowing
  thorns,

dagger hilt down into the throats of vines,
into the moat of darkness.

Waves of newborn light
quicken the dead stones;
the bright eyes of foxes
burn in my bones.

WEST CLEAR CREEK

1. Promise

I shall walk with water
I shall bend my head by Clover Spring
kneel in the long grass beside its creek
I shall arise and walk westward.

I shall stand in silence
at the Valley of the Willow
I shall laugh with my second name
and my steps shall be swift
swift as clear water.

I shall walk with beauty on my left hand
the changes of Meadow Canyon
I shall hold Buckhorn in my right
my feet shall flow between two mountains
the mountain of cedar
the mountain of black rock
and I shall sing
"the leaf of the earth is my leaf
and all that belongs to the earth belongs to me
the sycamore and his moonlit limbs
the ribbed edge of the plunging water
the water round stones
all things."

I shall rest in the sun on Cactus Mountain
I shall stand at last on the edge of the mesa
while birds wing over the yellow field
my eyes will be green like the river's water
and my hands will be heavy with praise
as the winter wind my voice will be clear.

2.   Prayer

May all things begin in beauty
and through the returning seasons
may I walk.

May I walk in November
giving thanks
in old age wandering on a trail of water
living again and lively.

May I walk
walk with water
with grasshoppers about my feet
alive in the litter
of summer spent leaves.

BEAVER DAM ON WEST FORK

I

A footbridge stable
over the sun speared creek
hugely rocked in the late fall air,
the leaves descending lately
paving the footfall havens
beside the life clear water
and the horse pounded path.

I go overland in easy stages,
express of the mind that is journeying
into the high unechoed walls
of sandstone rusting,
wasting into the dateless and plenar future.

My foot impels my mind
upward in the remembered climbs
of Redwall and the single Hermit
of the sheltered shale.

I am shadowed by the concave overhang
that touches the brightly ribbing water
whose flowing grows
from stream bank seepage
moss roses of tendril green
in the dark plush tundra
of cold soft stone.

The sky is only a less possible path
fenced by the rust orange boles
of pine in its prime
and the holdfast fingers of Gambel oak.

I make a gauntlet run through the razored
   reeds
of creekbed grasses and the barbed and
   berryless
ligaments of vegetative resistance
which gash and graze me till my blood whole
   heart
reflects the bewildering joy of a voyage
against the quiet and consuming current.

I wade and walk and curse
crashing through a Western woodlot
in all the leaf stripped dazzle of a December
   snow
till the sky becomes the Way.

Shoeless, I force
incremental repetitions of the voyage,
Homeric wanderer to the narrowing realms,
to the vision of the skull
and the earth-eyed slit of light
shrinking from above.

II

All my stumbling force converges
to the point and prick of life

9

whose barbels bite and sting
and whose rocks roll sullen
from under my arched and disengagéd bones.

Now my damn has become a dam,
a holding movement in the war of time
against a splash of rolled stones
into the silent tarn.

Though surprised by the sound,
I recognize and respond
to the naive authenticity of the beaver's dam,
a bridge for thought and foot,
which I, devout in my pilgrimage,
step lightly over.

And then to kick with my naked foot
and disengage from the offended fern
the rabbinical skull of a rank toothed rodent,
some father beaver whose son now sculls this
  basin
and lies, newly alert,
under the thatched dome of his littoral home.

So that was what I heard,
the percussive slap of his tail
spanking the silence into
ambiguous and re-echoed flight;
not the slide of stones,
but the covering swirl of reflecting waters
over the wildness of his swift descent.

10

I stand
while the wilderness waters converge again
and the rock walls shudder into stillness
and the light of morning is composed.

III

What praises then for the iconed peace
of the reflected sky,
for the muraled walls of winter stone
cold under the cut of the canyon wind.

The stiffly searching pines
seem to have been stood up for the moment
by life's drive for the dying light;
I am alive as these bones are dead and living
    again
in slick wet fur and yellow incisors.

Yes, Yorick, I knew him, but not well,
and can never know what his socket has seen
nor the forbidden life of that Eden world
from which man, in his reason,
is forever defended.

ANTELOPE WASH

From a saddle south of Doney Mountain
we descend a slope below limestone ledges
cross thin grass and cinders
the silt of wind-strewn ash.

Nothing quite so white
as the thigh bone of a steer
at the edge of a one-seed juniper.

As the rock beds fossils
so this sand keeps
coyote tracks, deer prints
and the cleft ploddings of cattle.

Wherever winds have doomed cinders
to this midden arroyo,
we find a record of mixed scat—
cow chips, rabbit pellets,
badger and bobcat dung.

Tumbleweeds
block vacant burrows
where the green of Ephedra burns
beside pale husks
of last season's saltbush
and the clear whistle of a Say's phoebe
hovers the high desert air.

Where a side canyon cleaves the rim
the sun shafts down
from a prairie
of winter-lost pronghorns.

Now light fails in the overhung shelters
seedless, without water,
and a cottontail outdistances us
to a dry falls.

Here the wash ravines
to sandstone shards,
silt from Moenkopi's
shallow sea.

In the fullness of sight
these signs testify
to numinous beings
whose numbers exceed the real.

We walk through patterns of the past
toward a present darkness
in which the sky springs open
and coyote sings
his eyes wide
to the light.

ON THE TRAIL TO RAINBOW BRIDGE

My foot follows the snow water
of February's end,
while my mind is impressed
by the love-worn curve
of wind-honed stone
varnished and limned
by the slow freehand of time.

Clearer than my human thoughts,
the stream bed under the winter sun
speaks nothing of dread,
nor of rage,
nor of the thrust of mud and brush
torn in the storm passion of a moment.

The bars about the sometime pools
speak of the spoor of deer
and of their clustered scat.

Here it is hard to believe
that all cries are of love,
the ordered rage for knowledge,
or the cries of the flesh in summer dress.

Here is none of the hot joy of sound;
only the season's stillness

with its whispered life
like the surge of distant falls
and their seethe and fade.

The melt from Navajo Mountain
sinks through intrusive stone
as its plateau
utters pine in hip-deep snow;
crossbedded, the canyon below
declares in weathered bas-relief
shores ancient beyond belief.

Castellated spires, knobs, thumbs, and domes
carve and splay
the sea-gray sky of fading day,
while the ribbon of river-green lake
demarcates the old orange and antique pinks
  and grays
of cliffs whose cornices are peeled
from the onion dunes of buried bays.

Everywhere under my feet
stone surrenders its transient form
to the beaten path that upward leads
past tentative formulations of the arch,
visioned and ever expected,
whose giant red rock thighs
straddling the undercut of Aztec Creek
I've come to see.

The bridge stands
archetypal and clear—
even to the carelessly observant
matter is informed with principle
and marshals beauty in inhuman ways.

Whatever intellect inheres in nature
seems satisfied at this moment with an arch—
one that provides no thoroughfare for man.

There is a homely silence that prevails
in this fretless atelier of natural law—
for all its patent workings, industry,
only the patient evidence of wind.

Philosophers, theologians, forgive me,
if I, through arches of socket bone,
recognize affinities
with arched and ruined stone.

2 / ORIGINS

STEPS, NOT TO BE TAKEN

I cannot say I counted them myself,
for some were broken down and some were hid
by scrubby thicket oak and chaparral;
but they were steps and led straight up the
  hill,
and I would count them if I could or get
lashed by an oak tree or my trousers torn.
So up I climbed, counting the ones I could.
        Let others slide,
I told myself, for numbers by themselves
are meaningless beside the mystery of
who built these steps, then left the hill to take
them back into her brambly arms again.
So much that passers on the road below
have never guessed that stonework steps are
  here
leading from nowhere to nowhere.
Yet once there was intention in the eyes
of those poor fellows, more than one, I guess,
who shoveled sand and lifted rock and swore
that no one should be to-building in a place
twenty miles from any house or town.
        And partly right they were, for though
the people now, in cities, press this hill
and on its crest the master's mansion frowns,
its roads, the ones that lead up and depart
go off in serpentining ways and slip

down the far slope into the stream of things.
But never within a rifle shot of where
these steps begin and end, as if they stood
waiting for the world to come to them.

WAR AND THE UENO ZOO: TO THE TIGER

*(During World War II all carnivorous animals in the
public zoos of Japan were destroyed and replaced
with farm animals as an economic measure.)*

Assuage indignities, can death do that?
Nobility must fall when kings descend!
We, not surprised that War has such an end,
must mourn your passing, great king-hearted
   cat.

Park deer Imperial, the light foot herd
and musical among the short-cropped grass
that hints the hooved impression as they
   pass—
Why must you go when these remain
   unstirred?

You, bent tired tiger, with tired tiger eyes,
pad up and back your cage in figure eights
and do not know the favor of those Fates
who spin and count and cut. Your honor dies

While pigs and sows and shoats, domestic
   things
who never knew the glory of the hunt,

befoul your caged dominion with a grunt—
these are the things expediency brings!

22

LINES AT A LEPROSARIUM

First, careless etchings of endemic rash,
Then failing sensitivity to touch,
Frostbite without a frost, a death disguised
By surgeon's gowns and Latin terminations
And prevalent as dust on empty shelves.

There are a hundred ways to pass the gate,
To enter that one road that leads away.
Ask all the many who in boarded rooms
Cough, bleed, and cry consumptive nights on
    end.
Thin voices still reproach the empty air,
Awaken sympathy in those who hear,
But sensitivity inures at last.

Concerning Death, conceptions contradict.
Some wait in earless silence for His step;
Some watch through sightless windows for His
    sun.
Cat's cradle is a game the children play,
Then stop to hear the plum rains in the pines
Or watch the yawning goldfish in the pond
That flick each fin in circular existence.

They wonder at a life so circumscribed,
Forgetting that their garden, too, has walls,
That human limbs may swim in bottled rows

As learned and labeled evidence of death.
They do not know that wrinkled, pickled feet
In jars of uniformly bluish green,
Suspended in the act of dissolution
And parted from their proper dust, may rest,
As postscripts to forgotten funerals.

THE SWIMMER

The tide pools at her feet
as she turns from the broken-oared dunes
the salt lick of a forehead curl
over her face.

She leaves behind
the spear strong autumn grass
to lift churning legs
through the white cascade of her shoulders.

And swims under the moving shadow
of each trough swiftly
outward bound toward the arbiter
of lost sailors
and the sea lion's stone gaze
to become a weed brown spot
on the sea rose navel
which the ocean embraces, erases,
the long clouds hinged against the sky.

Lost in the distant blue
far white tumble incoming
riding the outward flow
she spreads the level sea
holy as the dolphin
secret as deep solitude

a diminishing light
to herself alone.

No longer languid
in the strong light
she minnows sharply
all restless seaborn tense
strikes for the gone land
till the water lords lift limb
through swells green-bluing
and surf boards her forward helpless
onto the heaving sand
shrinking
breathless
and restored.

ALL MUSIC HAUNTS ME

young rabbits run
over the sunrise lawn
of the Catholic cemetery
on a ridge that looms
above the Huron
heron valley
below the smoke blue hills

the great beaked bird
her rippled staring
into the sunlight waters
oily in the heartbreaking air
rising over the cat-tailed marshes
where a redwing rides
a reed stem
and cuts the day with his cry

a green morning
when a hawk on point
circles the valley
with ascending wings
and gathers force
in a flood of sun
that dazzles and drugs

the dun owl scowling
from the dark river wood

all music haunts me
inhabits my dawning

THE FAR SHORE

I sail close under a lee
On an unstrange sea,
With the far shore's intangible charade
Seen in parade
Of silhouette and changing cloud
Continually made
On the turning spit of the sun.

My sail fills well and the wind is firm;
The buoy dips
In the running wakes of seaward ships,
And I hear the bell.
Wind's flaw, cat's paw, and the dimpled sea
Casts off his spell,
And I lift one wetted finger to the wind.

Wondering at the word the tell-tales bare,
Trembling there,
Heading me, backing me, changeable now,
Who knows how?
Strength and direction ride the air,
Till it comes again fair,
And I sail with my back to the wind.

TRANSCRIBING THE TAPES

The voice has a familiar ring—
the class ring of twenty-three.
Perhaps there is music on the far side,
a march at best for old soldiers
who are the best of fathers.

It is his voice remembering that I hear,
The pauses, the chuckles, the laughter
that interrupts itself.

Giles Grady and the canvas canoe,
the Mississippi landings
like Sam Clemons his-self,
musing on the past
neither heroic nor romantic,
just past, long past.

An upright piano
that bleeds keys
but unlocks no doors.
The iron prod of a rail
along the small of a boyish back
that rode the forbidden rails
and the loose gravel
lie to his mother.

The quarter from under the couch
that rolls into a cap gun,
with a volley of ordinance
that is not ordinary,
no more ordinary than
the pausing voice
that is his.

This voice of mine could go on
singing a litany of things done,

but that voice,
his voice
is still.

LINDISFARNE

The long waves that lifted
their serpent bows
now shock the headland
of tidal rocks
and roar in the recesses
bearded and trembling
like timid scholars.

South sailing
over the whale-road
their dragon ships
have entered the Tyne
skimmed the spit
at the mouth of the Tweed
homed on the swells.

They have come
in quest of sword take
a cunning of coins
franked with the face
of a smiling Caesar
or female captives
for trade on the Vistula.

Come with a curse
like a gull's high cry

from that berserk Bjorn;
their oars are shipped
with a clatter of bones
their shields unlaced
from the handworn gunnels.

The cleric stirs
in his pious sleep
for this is his dream.

ORIGINS

Note calls note, compelled by force to follow
In order half concealed by pounding feet,
The mandolin, the fiddle, and guitar.
We allemande and star, and unaware
We tread upon a heritage descended
From Appalachian hillside isolation,
From half remembered Surrey and old Kent,
We turn and circle with the riding sun.
Here is no pole of green nor do the Druids
Wind in their serpentine to hymn the stone.
No sacred oak, no sun's fertility,
No Hobbyhorse to whinny death away—
The common then was holy for the shepherds
Who turned in singles round the Sheepskin
  Hey
And rubbed their Saxon knuckles, red with
  frost.

3 / EARLY RISING

THE LONG RAIN

The brightening is slow
the pines are black
in the morning glow
light seeps earthward
earthward from the sagging cloud.

She stirs in the arms of dream
stirs, sighs,
and sleeps again
faint on the rooftop
rain.

Soft steps to the kitchen
a door cries, a faucet coughs
Saintpaulias are watered
while eggs set
and bacon shrivels
shall it be coffee and grapefruit
she wonders
or chocolate and sweet rolls?

She stands at the window
arranging the leaves of the ivy
subdued to the mood of the morning
the teacup seems to float
on a pond of polished cherry

red as old blood
or the dying sun.

She stands surprised and strange
at the sight of a rabbit
gaunt and motionless
against the long green
of the lawn.

How sharp and sudden is the desire
to hold its wet gray wildness
to her breast—
but the oven is warm
and ready for the rolls.

SAND POINT ELEGY

Her bones lie on the beach
open to the careful sun;
though at the edge of the sea
they seek no secrets.

She grew up accepting life as it was,
the cold rain crossing the dunes,
the sorrows of the old,
the shipless.

The sun comes down to the long sand;
every day she was born
of that sun and taken by the sea.

There is no blame in these bones
the tide returns.

GONE

Gone
sailed up the long lake
past the deserted island
the crescent sand.

Our love
that great self-centered
tenderness
seems to have charmed
the waters
as we ride the wind swell
the bow dipping lightly.

Up the prose-poem lake
its frosted edges
sun bare rocks
weed washed barrens
sedgy shallows
trout cold
set in a high
alpine wilderness
of whitebark pine.

Our destination
wolf meadow
and that high point of land

with its tower view
of the spent arrow serpent lake.

The rumpled skirt of the half-furled sail
lies in your lap
my bright and lovely.

The rudder is shipped
as the long keel grooves the sand
and you move naked
through the waiting water.

We have landed and the land is ours
the simple fire at dusk
the long light parting
the thin smoke
mornings of wave sparkled
wind and hunger.

There is another island
farther north
consumed by travel
we shall never age.

COASTAL DREAM

In cliffs of sleeping stones
in canyons of falling rivers
in bent trees
that claw the crests
of the drowned
and hay-stacked
ocean remnants,
the dream resides.

Among the small
smooth stones
of Agate Beach
the dream is lost.

In the sand
the winter surf
wipes clean
the dream is found again.

END OF AUGUST

I

The wind has promised us a dry September
when there shall come with dawn an ancient
  song
following the paths that die after August
through homes of locust and the hurried ant
at work in the harvest sun.

Each place we choose to wander
the summer sun has sweetened,
and the ceaseless pulse of the river
sings with the swarming gnats.

Let us walk the right of way beside
the straggling pines upon the slope
to where the wintering crows will come.

II

Solidagos have gilded the banks
we searched for fledgling robins,
and the meadow grass grows brown
despite the thunder.

Let us walk to the river to find
an oaken pail in the ryeweed thicket
and what few berries the catbird missed.

While watching the towering clouds to the
    west,
we shall ask:
"Do you think that's thunder?"
And we shall row at leisure
up the Great Chain river
to Constitution and the apple farms.

Following the trail to the fallen Redoubt,
we shall linger for sunset and on our way
    homeward
harry the grouse from his havening pines,
startle the fox at the foot of the spring.

III

Summer thoughts shall circle through our
    minds
upward toward the star of morning,
slide and sail like red-tails in the sun.

The fogs of morning wind through our woods
and the crows have collected to circle and cry
in the sleep-breaking dawn,
in the mists on the Hudson
that harbinger snow.

Our sill is splintered by the boots of strangers,
by fruits of welcome and by leaves of wine
and the dooryard path is worn and weedless,

for summer has burst with a boom of feathers
under the slope of the woods at dusk,
and our house is still with the quiet of waiting.

MOUNT HAMILTON

neither fern lake nor sharon hill nor the
  abandoned wagon
      fiddling in rust time against the parley
          of crickets
but hamilton range   a setting

daring the adamant signs
      plucking the barbed wire
          skirting the thin ponds
they place their tent under the pine trees

fog hides the hill nor is it exorcised by childish
  wit
        and tracing back the pocked and cloven
          path
          of stupid sheep
they recollect the fire   the wood   of a simpler
  day

fording a spring and hurdling the wagon ruts
        they tread the sharp grass
            while memories   bay leaves   burn in
              the mind
and rebellious horses narrow the way back

THE ROUND SEA

At the round sea's uncertain edges
The rock dust gathers in rest
And we look down from the winter hedges
When you and I surmount the crest.
Catching the sea dust in our eyes,
We wait for the tide to rise.

First lean from the west, arrowed and planed,
Then liquid and full, the wind will swell
Climbing the hills it has obtained
Or caught in the ear of a conch's shell,
While you and I listen still
To the surf's running and the waves' spill.

EARLY RISING

The mink returns from his midnight prowl
And the fox at dawn on the frosted hill
Stands to the call of the black oak owl;
The grouse in the woods are still.

The sweet recorder music of the birds
Whistles the daybreak to my ear,
Hymning and ending the resting hours.

Full of the savor of spring
And the sap of young times
And the breath from the wind-strewn river,
I drink in awareness and rise.

4 / OLD HOUSE, OLD YARD

PONDEROSA

51

Some windows of the sky are open
so dawn can find
our last porch step is missing,
sunk in the night
by a searching drift of snow.

Weather-wise, a plow is working,
a dirty-yellow vessel,
with strawberry lights to starboard,
whose bow
curls a breaking wave
on the snow-stripped beach.

I take to the tundra of Birch
following its frozen wake,
a Black-footed penguin
and solitary as Admiral Byrd.

Under sagging wires the city sleeps.
A slipping roof of snow is seamed like dough,
and at corners the high crossed signs
have lost their green.
Every street is White Street
it would seem.

The city trees are suffering;
in every block their April branches,

budded and blown, are down—
white wounded boles
above massed falls of limb.

But roving west along a road
of bowed and stricken elms,
I reach the always summer pines.

They speak in their accustomed stance,
their canted boughs
clear of the staggering drifts.

I rest against a splattered bole,
bark wet and white
where the clustered flakes
link arms.

On a snail's run of pitch
a needle clings head down;
lifted by my eyes,
I lose the common ground.

GATHERINGS: SWITZER CANYON

1.   Sticks

Repeated raids have made familiar
the unposted edge of the lava cap
broken into monolithic shards,
tumbled clay from the earth's innards,
stone sludge from the solar maw.

It is private land—somebody owns it—
a corporate entity, a legal abstraction,
has taken the deed
then left it to me
and meadow mice
and the quick, gray fox.

Their minions maimed a road,
began another and quit,
spit in a ditch bloody cinders;
the ponderosa dies in piled sections,
russet heaps beside white stakes,
orange streamers.

Cottontails haunt them,
safe refuge for a month,
deceptive haven;
they know no other enemies.

Now I have come as a predator
to take by stealth the ready wood,
a thoughtful despoiler, foregatherer of tokens
and elemental imagery.

The gash heals to a sick scar,
the wood welted from the cat's claw,
the iron of invention that cuts and bellows
as development casts its long-green shadow
like a witch's curse.

Nothing gathers to a shade
along the havoc path;
a vulture, a pale profiteer,
I pick the bones, gather the leavings—
simple firewood to return its former suns
to me and mine.

Each carload makes, I tell my wife,
enough to burn a witch or warlock,
while the land, staked out,
waits like one of Foxe's martyrs.

I would warn the world's body here,
could it take warning,
had it place to run;
but only the sun moves in its heavenly languor.

Back with the stacked limbs,
I bring the sharp joy of form—

split rock, dense shade, oak thickets,
occasional fir.

An indigenous nation here,
all ages and conditions,
pine is their language,
needle and bough a breaking gesture;
their maimed monarch, with beetled branches,
has abdicated in favor of death.

"Trees," I think, "only trees,"
as their thick bark,
curved to the bone it covered,
lifts in my hand,
sluffs off like charred skin from the arm
of a dead child.

In a sawdust of insect rivings,
the wood beneath is tunneled
by long-horned beetles,
by wood ants a thumbwidth in length.

Larvae in their ghostly sheets,
the copper sheen of a pupa case,
proclaim that tree fellings
are really resurrections.

My gleanings follow the waste of the unready
    road,
a saw-cleared, sun-filled way,
sky-catching, contrailed.

The larger boles will wait
for my Swedish teeth
and my hurried strokes,
for the mole hills of men are mounding nearer.

The red saw rests,
breath steadies the pulse;
no mirrored illusion,
each log lady's cut in two,
then carried, chest or thigh,
stumble-footed down the slope
back to the stationed wagon.

I rest on a rock,
reptilian, sluggish, professorial,
till sun's heat frenzies my brain
and my blood skitters through oak leaves
like a horned lizard.

Songbirds in my head,
I go prancing like Pan,
feeling my earned fire
hot as an ant in my mouth.

I dance homeward with treebones,
my shade-lovely loot,
neglected leavings.

2. Stones

The government's forests are mine already
(rite of birthright, blessing of citizenship)
but gathering there requires a permit;
what a bank owns, unfenced, accessible,
is everybody's too, but with this difference—
there is no one to ask permission of
when trees are felled for fungus food
or lichened stones left boldly lying.

The stones were for landscaping—
here there were too many,
on my lot too few;
I began to set the balance right
by lifting them from their random beds.

In the hollows underneath,
a panic of ants,
the quick coil of a centipede,
the shrinking and burrowing
of a light-struck larva;
clinging to the undersides,
cold spiders
or the white gauze of an egg case.

Rocks lie everywhere in the grass,
ice-cracked, sun-split, summer-broken;
each a lichened beauty
gray green, flecked with orange or russet.

Descending the rubbled slope,
a rock in each hand,
earth-smudged and savage,
breathing deeply,
I thought "No fences make poor neighbors,"
hoarding the green gold of curved stone
like dwarf's gems in all shapes and sizes—
hammerhead, jawbone, dinner plate, shield,
spear point, teapot,
toadstools of splendid stone,
chips from the mesa,
its high, crumbling edge
a complex entertainment for the eye,
fox crannied,
colored by jay screams and hawk shadows.

My instinct for esthetic form
recognized each welcomed stone;
knees bent, hands grasping opposite edges,
my stomach lifted each into a more civil world,
a corner lot where a raw house stood in fill.

"Only half a mile," I said,
"there'll be pines and a garden hose
to keep your lichens bright";
each kept its stony silence
even as the rear springs sagged
and we moved in low.

Bones aching, palms abraded,
I rest from another load;

in the night I sleep soundly,
stoned.

By day the land lies waiting;
and loving as I stole, blessing with my thought,
I knelt in reverence on a natural altar,
the profaned hillside—
everything done by hand
in a grave silence
under a grave sun.

Machines will condominium this slope,
highrise the pines into a hundred residences—
the piston will not bend to kiss the rock
nor plow blade make apology.

Hillside under the winged sun,
you wait quietly,
dreaming nothing,
fearing neither the devil's dynamite to come
nor the witch's whine of the saw.

I alone feel guilt.

LINES ON THE DEATH OF INKWELL

1.
Alive he would not have fitted into any box
this small
but a brown paper bag from the supermarket
might have held his curiosity
for a moment.

He would leap
from the kitchen floor to his place on the
   counter
at the first squeak of the can opener,
the black triangle of his fox face
streaked with an evening elegance.

Later,
He would not stir to my step.

Though we tried force-feeding,
in the end we could not keep him going—
whipped whole eggs,
Gerber's High Meat turkey,
even science's holy wafer
the Unipet Vitamin,
all were in vain.

His platelets running ragged
had killed his taste—
he did not care to eat.

Little by little, less by less
he grew inward, awkward,
dying in our helpful hands.

Before the plasmodia darkened
the fire in his pulse and brain
his eyes mooned green and giant;
and his death distinguished him
from the litter he was born to.

2.
Our back fence dandy
had yet to catch his queen—
instead some tainted finch
his instinct's sureness caught
taught him a blacker dream,
learning death is a maiden
with soft paws.

By sunset he'll be packed away
like Christmas ornaments
filed below hollyhocks
in the backyard clay.

(One ear keeps flipping out
of his cardboard coffin
as if to listen and scoff
at our fractional tears,
our marginal losses.)

As the living do with the dead
we remember the beast cry
of his courtyard conception,
and the dull red
of his pencil eraser nose.

And we wonder
is this prevision or perversion
that death draws us to life,
that we loved him more
in his dying weeks
when his fur hung on him like a shawl
across the shoulders of a feverish child.

3.
Our children,
who delight in a cat's simplest gesture,
will bid him goodnight tonight,
will fare their wells to his fever-found grace,
his low crouch in the forbidden grass
and upward spring like a split-end
caging a locust.

I shall tell them he's returned
to the natural gardens of fact and fate
and to celebrate
I shall write them a poem about a cat
about Colleen and Uncle Remus
and Fern and Wilbur
with lines quick as cat silver
streaked black as a ditch.

But the children will be home
and I must show them
the communal notoriety of their pet
who, disfigured by his death
and folded like old clothes
into a depression suitcase,
is there, here,
enshrined.

POND WATER: THE MICROSCOPE

I

I sought it, bought it, grew
astonished at its beauty
poised on my study desk
angular and true.

Though no lens
truly compensates,
it did its best,
and under its eye
always objective
I pieced things out.

One-eyed I sat and considered
Cyclops the leaper
and Cladocera
Euglena and Paramecia.

Seeking illumination
I fixed each there
in the condenser's upward stare
under a cover glass
on a well slide.

II

The pipette leaves another drop;
I watch a roll of diatoms

and algae like the lights
of passing ships.

Dazed by iridic dance,
I descend, shrink to a seed shrimp sculling
and rest on the dark ground—
light's angled incidence
resolves what mysteries it can.

Two-eyed, I sit and consider
why I died
my curiosity still
unsatisfied.

III

Though manweaver
at the heart of his web
extends his senses,
his is still
the world of a glass jar
on a window sill.

Instrumentally slain,
strange learning steels us;
Pasteur has left the room
to wash his hands.

HOUSE MOUSE

Shattered, his bead-black world,
the length of tail all twitching,
stilled.

The tiny, fleet feet that moved him,
blurring in an optical feint
along the wall behind the Simmons couch,
now bedded to lie, still and stiff,
under a litter of needles
and loose brown dirt;
beneath a sandstone headstone
upright as the balloon gray ears
once cupped to the sound of my steps,
inquisitive at the gnaw
and crumble of the fiber walls.

My instinct was to spare him—
anthropomorphisms were in order,
not only for the children's sake
but for my own,
steeped in the views of the naturalist
and convinced
of the magnificent unity of life;
and his, mammalian and hot-blooded
as the softly fleshed bones
of my wife.

To set a trap to take a life
an easy thing; but, careless,
the trap went off in anger—
no, not at me,
but at its mission,
I projecting into the neutral contrivance
my own and murderous guilt.

Sharp cheddar and the soft
release of the spring against
the trembling catch.

It held, like the poised heft
of the guillotine against
the cable's unutterable release.

In a shredded nest of reasons
I hid the act;
mouse damage, mouse dung
hung like a moral odor
beneath the trussed up sleeping bags.

He had to go,
and I and the children took him, singing,
on the broken necked trowel
and smoothed the anguished peaceful eyes,
and named him Morris,
conducting him to a colder home.

OLD HOUSE, OLD YARD

I

His impulse ran wanton
to the top of the street;
he had not forgotten the old house.

Cheepy birds still brushed the boughs
of the twenty 'leven trees;
limbs from the elms still split above the grass.

He sought the petrified wood
too old to inflict the sentimental curse—
all else was charged with time.

II

He saw how the weeds plumed high,
their panicles blown and cast;
still scorched was the August stump
through fumes of fire.

He stared at the dog worn spot
now gone to clover and the clover gone
and was a source for the rinsing fire of life
watering the withered sod, the worm poor
  earth.

He pitied the unbedded wastes for flowers,
the shade sick four o'clocks,
and the finger nipped buds
of the flare orange drooping fern of poppy.

Under the old regime that mint expired
and the questionable fungi throve—
how many times had the lilac aborted,
one spring only to purple the lawn!

III

He knew the primly mincing skunks
under the leaping steps
at the sun dead hour for watching
the city lights or feeding
summer spiders.

He stood beside the peach tree
of American painted ladies
and thought of Mourning Cloak
and the patient cementing of twigs
and how her larvae had vanished
in a single night of rain.

About the shrunken shed
horned lizards, hawk on a pinehead,
and from the unsteady terrace stones
the stealthy fingered walk
tarantula.

IV

Beneath the ball thrown hoop
he felt his wife at war;
inside the lockless door,
an ax at rest, a crown of antlers.

He sealed the winter sashes,
wove spring wire into the pricking screens,
and nosed the carton's corrugated wet and curl,
mildew, and the sick odor of summer dust.

He found spent cartridges on the clay sill,
abandoned webs in the boarded windows,
old pieces of pipe,
a rope tied to a rafter.

V

He paused at the northeast corner,
pondered Morris his bones,
burned sticks washed out on the bald ground.

Paper plates curled in the picnic fire,
franks hissed and blistered,
the center of his mind marshmallow soft.

He touched the niched and ivied walls,
the frayed and tumbled cones;
flew again the flimsy craft
till it crashed in the brooming pines,
and the plastic parachutist dangled,
lord of what dies.

VI

But if there were roaches by night
there were robins by morning—
and children, always children.

He hummed:
*twice around the island
twice around . . .*

He knelt, lifted
the unembittered stone,
and wept.

5 / JOURNEY TO THE INTERIOR

HART PRAIRIE HERDER

"Ein Tausend," he had said,
Iladio, in his broken German—
but Spanish was his tongue;
Spain his country.

He knew the days of the week,
the months, the simple words;
could count to twenty—
"Kein Englisch . . . ein Jahr in Amerika."

We talked
while his black and white Pachuco
whirled in his joy,
tore at his diminishing tail,
its white blaze instantly
out of his teeth.

Our family had come to Wedding Ring Tank
seeking the lost emblem
of my bondage,
the earth circle.

But spring-fed it swayed
wind-rippled
and undiminished through the summer
  drought
the swallows knew it.

"Hier ist es sehr schön," I said
the land gentling down,
a brook below,
Sitgreaves in the distance.

I thought, too, as I spoke,
of our bodies entering here,
making their own circles within
the circling pond;
the giant pine silent
as the silver band slipped from my finger.

Pachuco spins again
and, ringing with laughter,
the children hug his gentle fur,
snatch at his scything tail.

Iladio nods. *"Mein Hund, vier Monaten."*

Our greater family stands
in the half light falling
from a Pan's space of sky
above the hills' volcanic softness.

I think he must know herding songs,
lulling tunes with words
sad as the Spain of Cervantes,
noble and gentle, and simple as his face.

The robin twilight closes—
Pachuco might be taken for a skunk;

swallows still ring the sky,
dip and rise.

He breaks a stick in his friendly mouth,
then drinks at the water's edge
where the rocks are streaked with droppings
and the clay is clumped and cloven.

"Perro, vaya con Dios."

The shepherd hears and smiles.

Iladio,
affection for your dog
has joined us,
and if we knew
the old songs of fellowship,
we would sing them,
married as we all are
to the earth.

FULL MOON ON GOVERNMENT PRAIRIE

The rising moon at dusk
offers these hills its light
in return for their shadows.

The small dog of the prairie
is free in his love,
and when coyote can no longer see day's face,
he seeks night's fullness.

If coyote were to ascend a hill
to a summit with cairns as clears as light,
if shadows were to follow him,
the forms of elemental things
would dazzle the vastness behind his eyes.

Let the amber of his eyes
mingle with the diminished light
of the brightest stars
while the moon lights a campfire
between the stark hills
and the great spiral in Andromeda.

THIS SLANT OF LIGHT

This slant of light
lengthens the stance of junipers,
gilds the leaflets
of velvet mesquite
and its straw-colored pods.

The sun lies lightly
upon the leafless sycamores
and winter rain has greened
the meadow grasses.

Together we stand
beside the black intensity
of a boulder whose multiple faces,
crusted by the lime and mustard of lichen,
are numinous from every angle.

We have no time to divine
its minimal but enduring soul—
the karma of its incarnation
beyond understanding
in a world made of stone.

SPRING SAFARI

1. Long

Long Canyon's spring is vernal
below a gunsight pass
where shred-bark, blue-green cypress
guard the gates
that bleed below the canyon's rim;
their Chinese-puzzle cones
as inexplicable as nature.
Downstream an unseen wren
lets fall a few curved notes.

2. Fay

We climb a slope of broken slates
to an arch that frames
the white-throated cries of swifts
whose flight invites
delicate diptera.
Where Fay extends her arms,
we take her left hand close to the wrist
and climb to the island stone.
No paths bleed up the boxing canyon
to the shrub summits of Bear Mountain;
the ledge is all we have.

3. Secret

Though uncertain of the entrance
to Secret Canyon,
where we walk the thatched boles of yucca

seem grossly familiar,
flame-headed ants frenzy
over the earth's fine grit,
and shield bugs edged with orange
meet in a backward embrace.
Above the manzanita's massed devotions
overwintering leaves and twisted limbs
green the Supai hills.
Three times we circle Grassy Knolls,
the buckthorn breasts of Changing Woman;
a fine rain falls,
dries on our faces.

MONSOON SUMMER

Names add little to our knowledge;
we know only the things our senses bring—
trees and their leaves,
clouds, rocks, and fungi.

Wet to our knees,
we tally mushrooms
fragile stemmed and darkly gilled,
running to creams and russets,
tans and browns.

The rain has taken our clothes;
our thoughts have turned to mold;
we come from caves,
our limbs are firmly fleshed,
fibrous, striate, off-white.

Breathing an air of garlic, spice, and rose,
we grow in the rain of Hart Prairie
and know the ephemeral nature
of our fruiting bodies.

MOSE CASNER ON HIS TRAIL,
JANUARY 1900

Wet Beaver runs clear from Brady Canyon to
    the Verde,
some of its waters channeled to fields and
    pastures
where blackberry brambles thicken
till a streak of blood bubbles
across his blundering knuckles.

About him the pulse of water
over red-rock ledges
and a chaos of bird song—
hosts of winter robins, tree-busy,
full of spring and call notes.

His cabin and corrals lie thirty miles
to the north of the butte
and canyon that carry his name.

His journey ends in the truth of White Mesa,
dies to game trails that branch and fade
like the purple veins on the back of his hands.

He looks up to slopes where cliffs of sandstone
buttress the canyon wall
and empires of prickly pear

consort with malpais and cholla—
when they catch the sun
their pods glisten like ancient rain.

Coyote has left the red-orange seeds
of juniper berries clustered on trail-side stones
and a felt of field mouse fur to mark his scat.
With wapiti and mule deer, Mose Casner
accepts this right of way.

Breathing hard on the trail,
he stops to salute the cirrus to the south
that tame the hatless sun
and cool the basalt bastions
above bare reaches of scree.

There is no name for the maker
of the cup marks on the volcanic stone of this
    promontory—
each filed with the clear melt of snow.
Heaped boulders lean toward the hollows at
  his feet
where night homes in on the day.

Everything he sees is either near or far;
there is no middle ground where he stands
at the last leap of this lava cliff,
while the calls of pinyon jays cleave the cold air
as their flocks scatter and converge and break
  again
like waves upon the shores of Molokai.

He knows there are names enough to cover this
    country,
Rarick and Mullican and Bell,
but these translations have eclipsed
the old Sinagua signs.

Even White Mesa is named for a man—
its grasses tawny from January nights,
its surface heavy with stones,
though the earth is still soft
from last week's storm.

He lifts his eyes to the snow
that frosts the Mingus Range
and clings to the north-slope gullies.
Everything is either near or far.

Mose Casner, age sixty,
ranches south of Flagstaff.
If he does not leave children,
he will leave his name
and horses...horses...horses.

JOURNEY TO THE INTERIOR

As we begin our descent
a girl on a black gelding
ascends into the light
of our collective vision.

Between boles of aspen
and boughs of Gambel oak
we sense the increasing depth
of the divided canyon.

Where an evening primrose glows
in a dusk of thunder
we dream of sun-mottled ledges
above a dark ravine.

Close to us
and close to each other
Chief Thunder speaks
for a second time.

Cornered in this canyon
between lava and limestone
we climb the trail
of yesterday's rain.

6 / A DISTANT HERON

THE VULTURES OF WALNUT CANYON

Some may sing of hawks and hunting falcons
or the wild swans of a remembered lake,
but there are other nobilities.

If we disregard
their unaesthetic but utilitarian
taste for carrion
and their brazen-necked
irreverence for the dead
as they sit on dust-road haunches
squabbling over peculiar bread,
we must admit they rise
to a height beyond our might—
things that cannot be better done by man;
their primacy is flight.

Look,
there on the peaks the cumulus rise,
a noon phenomenon repeated here
as, sun-sucked, the column air
soars as strong as pines
to gift the vultures
to their trembling sport.

I prize
the illusion of ease
and the unparalleled harmony

of an adaptation
old before man was dreamed.

I admire
their lift and spire,
the fingering spread
of the great primaries
upcurled in the drift and ruffle of wind
and the easy tilt and swing
of dark and light banded wing.

Cautious and controlled,
their cruise is endless in the noon;
without the faintest flap,
the rising canyon's breath
is caught and mastered
in a great volplane
and spiral infinite.

As they elevate the imperceptible current
and hawk high in a great arc
to hover on the apogee of noon,
their swart feathers splayed and rippled,
they measure the limestone canyon walls
whose time-baked muds reveal
the print of palm
fresh from the shaper's hand,
and, effortless, instinctive,
are above them all.

Banking in hollow-boned spirals,
they adjust, recoil, and temper,
the spring of each being taut
and infinitely professional.

I repeat,
it is the illusion of ease,
the parable of art;
and I have felt thus only
rare and infrequent,
at limb's length sprawled
in a lifting sea
or bellied upon the waters
below Mooney Falls.

And even if
all our lives could be swimming,
we, left-footed creatures
and martyrs to gravity,
could not attain,
could never attain to this.

LINDBERGH SPRING

I

I dip my hand into Lindbergh Spring
and red with cold
lift burning ladles.

A fistful of weed and substrate silt,
a skimming of lesser duckweed—
green rafts with simple moorings.

The scene settles overnight,
clears in a nine-pound jar
whose foliage is a rainforest canopy.

Bill Beebe's high jungle
clings to this sea's still surface,
lifts broad leaves above the savannah of shrub.

My mind is fired by this glassed dominion,
a waterhole so geographic special
its images burn like the mid-earth sun.

Spyglass in hand like Walden's old surveyor,
I straddle a volcanic ridge
and watch for ring-billed toucans.

Clouds from Cayey
in a running mist
touch Darwin's rich, organic litter.

Lifting his Corinthian shell, a snail,
mouth bubbling like Bumpass Hell,
oozes along a rootlet.

II

What denizen stalks
this jungle
of descending stems?

No Saint George's worm
weaving his tentacled self
and strangely at home in this underwater
    Eden.

Nor the black beetle who breaches
this Sargasso stillness;
nor the water mite bleached by lamp glare.

Vines from the Belgian Congo
frond in San Juan's trade wind,
and reveal, mummied in duckweed,
an aquatic insect,
a caddis fly larva
whose thin hands work the soil.

Only movement betrays his perfect guise
as he bumbles through the high, looped
  branches
and sun floods the glade like Simba's mane.

BROAD-TAILED HUMMINGBIRD

The bird has come
wearing the white clean whistle of a hum.
Wing beats blur
on the sill of day;

it darts to the hollyhocks—
a pause—but not for long,
broad-tailed spinner
of summer's song.

SPARROW HAWK

I

I found him on his back,
the belly feathers grayish white and buff.

A twig's forked spatula showed a lifted head,
a curve of beak gun-gray
beneath black eyes rimmed yellow
and filmed with summer dust.

He did not move.

II

Desiring to touch his death
as if it were my own,
I took him gentle in my finger tips.

He was soft, frail soft, and sun-warm limp;
dead but unmarked by the dart
which age, or illness of age, had aimed
to knock cock kestrel off his winged walk.

I, who have few plumes and little beauty,
fixed on the unfaded colors—
sun yellow his ruffed legs,
flight feathers like a darker night
(they seemed so, edged in running white),

the most was simple rust and black
woven into the ancient scales.

Though few birds ever die of age alone,
this was not sleep;
the slow transition had begun,
and the uninformed ant and beetle lounged
in the shade of a death just done.

III

I think I saw him once
hunched in the lee of a dying pine,
contracted in the cold and wet
of a dismal spring;
I thought then he would not live to slant
above the fields I labor in,
gaining a little and growing old.

Though August rains will shrink him to a rag
and sun shall see his whiter bone at last,
this should be known:
I placed him in a better way,
close at the foot of the elm between two roots,
shaded a little and alone.

RED-TAILED HAWK

The pine is tall, black, dead,
grooved by the bright rifling of thunder;
he turns
slowly
the sun strong on the stones of hills.

A bird of prey, of passage,
he cries to the April sky
as his shadow lunges
along lime yellow cliffs,
dips to a rubbled ridge,
ascends
returning above the sycamores.

He falls sword swift,
silent as sunlight,
scores on a ground squirrel
who's rent like a storm
torn tent
spangled with bleedings.

Easy out of the warring winds,
his keening hunt now over,
he preens,
poised as Apollo
underfeathers soft as the flesh of surrender
and talons curved like Turkish scimitars.

SPIDER WASP

In the core of the cave
was a threaded snare
where, loosely knit,
Pompilida trembled,
feigning a fit.

Spider-quick the widow came;
sure of her prey
she poised, supreme
in the efficiency
of her webbed machine.

She stalked a moment, considered its size—
a shark in a seiner's net;
and yet she knew
her poison would do
even a larger fly.

She struck to make it die—
or did she miss?
It buzzed its fill,
jiggled its feinting chance;
she joined in its dance.

And then with abdomen curled,
the long, blue wasp
embraced its prey,

paused to disentangle a final string,
and took to wing.

Fore-thinking instinct
suppers up her young;
her burrow is sealed,
her black wings glitter
in the sun.

A DISTANT HERON

I am here to trace
the faint flight track
of yesterday's heron
luminous in the vanished sky—
a sound that slips through the years
like fingers.

It is not the same music
a mountain sucker makes
grazing on stream stones,
but it is similar.

And I am not disappointed
to stand among willows
with my sorrow less than absolute
because the light is empty of wings
and a remembered bird.

I too have stoned a robin,
and I'm still learning what lengths
that guilt has driven me
to love all winged things
in my long forgotten grief.

But the great blue heron
is never sad or angry—
he thinks in the sun

of flying upriver
to wade in the pools
along its southward facing banks.

The alders he shall pass
will fail to overwhelm him,
though their shadows
be as long as morning.

Let him fly in the silence
of a leafless winter
above cottonwoods as old as Adam
and feel only the guilt
of a stone.

7 / SUNSET CRATER

MOUNT WING

"Lost: one magnetic dog
halfway up the stair
of purple pine and fir."

"Why do you say that, dear?"

"Because this hand holds something half alive
and white."

Wing Mountain comes and hums
discreetly the secret of the missing
(as he stands at the head of the highway)
other half.

(My god, not another family outing!
the family that hikes together . . .
amid 'forest clad' slopes with their
'marching' pines and 'troops of fir'—
it's hardly fair!)

and not, for reader's sake, a poem
about those Hong Kong dogs!

With their Janus-faced duality
of solid black and alabaster white
demonstrating
(Oh, let us demonstrate together!)

eternally
that likes repel and opposites attract—
an oriental unity
of good-devil, god-dog.

The secret is subjective.

"A matter of personal magnetism," he said,
hauling in the forward pass, on a dead run,
over his shoulder, just in the fingertips,
cutting to the sideline and scoring.

"And it takes other forms," she said,
thinking of her youngest son's attraction for
the perennial mystery of invisible forces.

"How does it work?"

"God knows," I said. "Some natural law
has been given a name; say gravity
and you won't be wrong."

So he took them along in his open shirt,
and I did not think to say,
'Your pocket's zippered, put them there.'
assuming perhaps their hold on him, his hold
   on them,
equaled the force of their polar binding.

The black one was a boy we decided,
following the standards of our dying century.

The white? Well, you tell me.

It was a hard, hot climb.
We puffed at every game trail,
skidded in the cinders,
fell down in the needles,
found handholds in the grass.

"Hold here!" I panted, hustling children
fore and aft and done in, frankly.
"The crest is close."
But no one wanted more.

All perched, half slipping, poised;
ate peanut butter grahams, lemon drops, and
   water.
Nutcrackers screamed shipwreck
from the masts of dying pines
then followed each other across the windless
   sky.
I kissed the wife and mother.
The children kicked holes in the hillside,
had 'fun'.

But the Black Dog was gone, we found
when we made the crater crest and looked
down into the long hollow, its meadow
and mire hole sink.

Satan's dusky familiar had gone
barking and snuffling among the cones

on the dead cone, along its
fireless flank, adrift in cinders
and soft forest duff—
vanished but always there,
the center of diverging, converging forces.

"How long will he last?" the eldest asked.

The lodestone base, I thought, not long;
the plastic shape forever.
(Magnetic fields so stretched
cannot unite such distant lovers.)

More than a scraped knee,
less than the loss of a Tigger,
it only showed that thirty years
of physical attraction
is not the same as love.

GRAND CANYON

They said it couldn't be Dug—
the U.S. Corps of Engineers had other projects,
was engaged in a terrestrial redistribution
or some bureaucratic boondoggling.

No,
not for used razor blades
as some wit
had it.

The environment had some . . .
had something;
whatever it was,
it was supposed to be enough.

If they Dug it with sufficient
g
   r
      a
        d
          i
            e
              n
                t
there was hydroelectric potential
(cf. Childs on the Verde).

Gravity is cheap compared to coal—
Black Mesa is not infinite,
but the waters, Thank God,
go on forever.

Turbines turn, $c^h{}_u{}^rn$,
electrons roar off in pursuit of
the Red Baron
ruddy kilowatt.

First, of course, was the appropriation—
so many dollars and sense
for the digging.
Estimated: 14 years
                    4 billion dollars

Probable loss of life
                              INSIGNIFICANT
when compared to the
benefits to the people.

So it was Dug.

If you drive eighty miles north
of Flagstaff
you can see it.
Cars with passengers
                              TWO DOLLARS.
Subject to INFLATION!

CINDER CONE

I, in my careful descent
displacing at each step
loose cinders on their downward course,
greet
the myriad pulsing feet
of children eager in assault
and heedless as a landslide
upon a cockcrow village
and just as sure,
stealing the king of the mountain home
in U.S. Keds and Jumping Jacks.

Thus, I reflect,
since that latest eructation
spewed the land
your fate is clear as rain,
a fast descent in sliding feet
from cone to peneplain.

DEADMAN'S WASH

Old Indian land,
it smells of sun
and of clean earth washed dead there
below a hut of stone and clay
gray in the branched arms of day.

A sunbent infant's shoe,
a flattened can,
fleece in a shattered fence,
mark our slow family trudge
in loose undisciplined lines,
the tall son leaping skittish.

There on the clay butte crumbling above the
    ringed world
in the desert palette dull red monotone of light
all things seen erode the heart away.

In the natural course of water
the wash is wasted,
in the natural course of time and water,
    worn—
and the children,
their sand prints small to my splayed treads,
are leading, following, still.

WET BEAVER CREEK

I follow a footpath
as faint as a line
drawn in darkness
to a garden of flagstones
set in grass above the inner gorge
where Beaver Creek runs
to mudstone, froth, and silt.

Though water in motion
fills the canyon with its presence,
I feel nothing of the creek's turbulence,
and my mind is as clear
as snowmelt in a sandstone pool.

A tower of rock like a Celtic brooch
captures the light,
and my thoughts hang in the stillness
like the stripped bark of a sycamore.

My joy is as unwilled as the yellow berries
on the stems of these leafless shrubs;
my happiness as easy as the dance of gnats
to the soundless music of their own mating.

Juncos settle in the bare mesquite,
and I know that mule deer

will descend at dusk
from Casner Canyon
to leave tracks in the trail
as thin as thought.

Pockets of water stand
on weathered limestone
where a gray fox drank
and left its scat.

Hiking back toward the setting sun,
I meet with news of our missing dog,
and the cupped shout of her name
climbs into the canyon
unanswered by sky or cliff.

Keen, unaware she's lost,
the keeshond waits for us at trailhead,
as calm as Casner Butte
and untouched by any sense of guilt.

The air is heavy with leaf rot
and the odor of rain-ripe earth;
the only darkness is shadow,
the mere absence of sun,
and the evening is full
of the promise of light
that runs downhill
like water.

SUNSET CRATER

Here there is no sea,
but the day is bright with the spill and hill
of the shore-homing wind like gusty waves
and I all but see
gray gulls break flight
at the rise of night
to scatter like seedpuffs
in the down-beach wind.

The sun on the crater snow
is like sea sparkle on brown sand,
and the rush and tug of the air
ripples the hair
on the freckled back of my hand.
It is evening without birdwings
as I stand
overlooking the long silences
of peopleless places
dark under the dropping sun.

Through windlashed tears, everywhere
great eye-blinding lengths of earth
so measureless immense
the single mind confronted
turns inward against the multiplicity,

appalled and shaken
at the manifest indifference of the sky
to the foredoomed manifesto of the peaks
which, breaking, seem to say,
I rise and stand, I stand,
while everywhere they fall and fade,
subside and flow away
like giant abominable snowmen,
rumbling their mindless protest
down to trembling talus
and creek bed barrows
and dying in the April hemorrhage
of their streams.

8 / MEDITATIONS ON THE HUNTER'S MOON

THE TAO OF THE HUNT

Before the Age of Eden
there were no priests or kings,
only mothers who feared nothing but pain
and like the lotus
were willing to blossom and grow,
delivering us each from the mud
of the dark pond.

Ritual scenarios
of the demonic and the divine,
archaic as the potsherd
and the oak that bears strange fruit,
released each actor from his actions
so the sons could become hunters
who sense both the beauty and the terror
of the wilderness
and who crouch in the blinds of unknowing
knowing it to be exactly what it is
and are deeply moved
by the beauty of animals
using the awareness of an empty mind
to feel what the deer is thinking today.

On the hills behind them
the lotus mothers sink into the rising of birds
and the fall of the sunset winds
where the creek drops into darkness,

and the deer come into the reach of forgiveness
as precious as mice and milkweed.

While the hunters lie in wait
the edges of their knives
thin to nothing
and the world speaks to them
in the language of water and grass.

Their wonder returns as joy
pure as handprints
in the clay of a cave,
and now mothers and sons
move beyond the dance of two
into the heart of compassion
creating, from the bark of a fox on the hill,
a mind like trees and stones
shining without reason.

<h1 style="text-align:center">THE DESERT</h1>

Why do you feel defenseless
in this slow place
where nothing threatens save emptiness
and the silence can be killed by a single cry?

This desert is the death of closure,
and here no trees confuse those issues
whose importance diminishes
like stone to dust.

A mountain without use
is made to be touched with the eyes closed,
and your impatience will not even lead you
to the nearest wash.

These stones are light sleepers
and their dreams are as faint as dawn;
their knowledge is as wordless
as wire bent-nailed to a board.

The silence asks only for your ears
in return for nothing;
it knows that the sun is just passing through
on its way to another star.

If the moon should rise
as the sun sets

you will have two shadows
and not know which one is yours.

For a third will be cast
by the stone of your childhood,
and not even the raven
can help you decide.

All these rocks crave redemption,
and they welcome the sun as a sister
who will lead them home
after a long and pointless journey.

Though water comes down from the mountains
it has never reached this canyon
where night fathers itself
beneath a sleeping snake.

If you will take twigs of sage
and build a small fire
the desert will seem large;
perhaps its light will show you where you are.

SEEING THINGS
"Not only can I see once more, but I also SEE"—
  Shiny Stone

some can see but are not seers—
odors arise from riverbed stones
like footsteps left in the night
by a falling star

is the scent of rocks
lying broken in the sun
like that of old roses?

and how naked their eyes must be
in the dark of this ignorance
with sleep, like water, around them

but there are those who can see
the marsh light in the dark
and feel the slow root reach of a rowan tree
under a spring of snow

sight has no certainties like the heart
and neither hawk nor heron will answer
the water's silence or explain

if they were to live below words
they might rest in a final vision
and never regret the stones in the river

NORFOLK ISLAND PINE

you are conscious
of two kinds of light

sun from the single window
slants through the hum
of the fluorescent fixtures

and I think you hear my voice
when I speak to you
just as your mind
counts my thoughts

the wind of this stale office
does not shake the boughs I touch
marveling at your lightness
your easy motion as you sway

one fern hand hovers
over the cradled phone

would you answer if I called you
on some midnight morning
of sleet and wind
you who have so many fingers?

DESERT DAY, DESERT NIGHT

The desert day and the desert night
each has caught the other's foot,
and they turn like stones
in a dream of wind.

Night's rising moon at dusk
offers the desert
its light
without a hand.

If the day were to descend a trail
to a wash with stones
as clear as light,
if the night were to follow,
both would mingle with the desert stars
with the moon as their mentor
between earth and heaven.

MEDITATIONS ON THE HUNTER'S MOON

come inside this poem
as freely as moonlight
enters your room
there is stillness
in the tops of the pines

come inside the cold
out there waiting
for the dark to rise

nothing is stronger
than the light of this moon
for it is not an animal
that will ever die

men, do not include women
in your fear of nature—
what you fear is the hunter's moon

blackbirds sleep
in the night pines
as moonlight falls
between these words

when man brings his melancholy to the hill
the hill knows only moonlight

I do not speak of the tears of things
or of their slender sadness
but of a moon that shines
with its own light

Bashō found moonlight
inside a frog
its belly as silver as smoke

moonlight falls like water
when water falls into a still pool
the moon glistens on the rocks
and the pines are silent

the consciousness of this hill
is like moonlight
which is not a dream
the order of this hillside
is like moonlight
on a great stone shape

shape is consciousness
and the hunter's moon
has a pleasant shape
but never forget
that the hunter's moon
has a dark side

when you entered this poem
the moonlight
entered your body

if you leave your room
you will find moonlight
inside the stones

you have left this poem
as you will leave your body
under the hunter's moon

9 / THE SEASONED LOVERS

WOMAN AT THE EDGE OF THE SEA:
A Thirty-Year Old Photograph

She sits upon the port gunwale
of a boat above the tide
and looks down the unseen shore.

Brow shadows conceal her eyes
so that we cannot tell
if she is truly pensive
or lost in a wordless reverie.

The blue curve of painted wood
is her temporal throne
bordered by needle-like leaves
that stream in an onshore wind
too slight too disturb
her quintessential stillness.

Beyond her in the bay
small boats bow to the wind
at their distant moorings.

Is she listening to her thoughts
or inwardly silent
so that she may distinguish
the sea sounds that surround her—

the distant spill notes
where the horizon cascades
in an unbroken line
beneath gray billows of cloud;

the whispered pulse
of the eddies of foam
that surge in the shine of the wind
at her polished feet.

The two songs rise to ears
secretive beneath blond curls
that halo a face whose
features are so perfect
our eyes discount their vision.

A watch glints gold on her wrist;
a ring with a tiny stone
graces a fourth finger.
We cannot fathom
their personal significance.

And the exotic, subtropical tree
whose foliage borders the print
puzzles us like the absence
of sand dollars, skate's eggs, and turban shells
lying in a wave-row all unhoused.

The camera has placed her
in a pose that might be a century old

instead of thirty years;
a knowledge that lends weight
to the pathos of her image.

We must listen and feel
as far and still
as she listens now
to surf-mist over unseen dunes,
and feels now
the faint proximity of the chalk thwarts
that frame her casual thighs,
before we learn that her face
reflects an absence
as absolute as happiness.

LYN ENTERS HER GARDEN

Fenced from the forest
she cultivates her plants,
flowers like pieces of sun,
roses and apple trees.

Within these walls
honeysuckle scents
the aspen shade
and a universe of life
rises to the touch of her hands,
the tips of her fingers.

Here she is one
with the wind and the weather
where white petals fall
lighter than a gull's feather
and day lilies bow
in a lift of wind
that comes from a sea
as distant as memory.

A FRAGMENT FOR LYN

You must have walked far
and looked long
to find the one piece
that fits into
the broken bowl
of stars.

A FEW OF THE THINGS YOU ARE

The mothering oak of a woodland thicket
The ancient juniper on Anniversary Hill
Hart Prairie in October
A Bach chorale, prelude, and fugue
A broad-tailed hummingbird in flight
Narcissus in the snow
The winter sun upon my face

COMING TOGETHER

we have come together
in a tumble of love
with nothing between us
but the nakedness of space
taken and released each other
just as the dawn shatters
the ancient cup of night
into shards of light

TEACUP AND CANDLE

this is a teacup
it hangs by its handle
this is a candle
it has no handle

the teacup hangs in the cupboard
hangs by its handle
the candle burns by itself

sometimes there is light
without enlightenment

his finger fits the handle
her light flows through the room

the candle is white as china
bone white as China
or is it England

the teacup sits in its saucer
it is time for tea in England
is this tea from China

the candle eats itself
in the dark that it softens with light
the dark has a piece of it
it is smooth and warm to his touch

the water boils in its kettle
a mist rises
the tea brews itself
the candle consumes the dark

its light has no handle
is this China
or is this England

he lifts the candle to his lips
its light is honey and tallow

high time for tea she says

the candle in the cupboard
the cup in the wax
it is a melting kiss

her cup has but a single handle
does he burn like the candle
and will he kiss the back of her hand

raising the cup to her eyes
by its dainty handle
she shows him the white
china of her teeth

her smile makes a small fire
in the bottom of his cup
light shimmers on the surface of their tea

he asks are we in China or in England
she answers the cup sits in its saucer
the candle burns of itself
give me your hand

their fingers touch across the table
the cup sits in its saucer
she smiles
the candle burns

A MORNING POEM FOR LYN

Your fragile mind is like a flower
    perhaps a columbine
held in a child's hand
    remote in time.

Seconds climb toward an eternity
    that is finite yet infinite
and each morning's light shows
    what the face of joy can do

to suspend the moment in an embrace
    that is timelessness itself
yet yields to the pressure of our presence
    beside and beyond each other's empty arms.

Our lips part to join again
    as dawn breaks its wave
across the warmth of flesh
    and the decked horizon

rises and falls with the pendulum
    of galaxies pulsing
against the swirl of space
    whose clouds delight the morning sky.

THE SEASONED LOVERS

In this, their second spring,
soon to become another summer,
they are not quite lost in each other,
having eyes for things besides themselves.

While in each other's company,
they see the chalk and sandstone
canyon towers, fissured cliffs,
and know time is not their enemy.

They delight in the discourse of a creek,
chilling as its waters are,
just as they do
in the chatter of a squirrel.

While they move in shadows
of their former lives,
they are glad to greet the sun-lit glades,
knowing this land is theirs to share.

Finding themselves
in thunder and soft rain,
the other's life becomes
more fragile than their own,

and their spring love is like
the unfulfilled petal

of a Woods' rose
that summer will bring to flower.

Long given to waves and sun,
the crystal ambience of coral,
she has come to taste the trembling leaves
and touch the wood-sweet scent of wilderness.

He loves the sweet demeanor of her ways
and wills to be, with all his tender craft,
her friend and woodland guide
through the uplands of this life,

hoping fall will find them on lava ridges
amid the leaf-sigh of sun-bright aspen
or upon shelving limestone
under pines grown amber in their age,

and that winter will come to season their love
with nights of swirling snow
and the brilliance of stars
strung through the halls of space.

10 / DRY LAKE ELEGY

A THIRD COMING

Perhaps the ceremony of innocence
is not wholly drowned.

Bundled against the bitter wind,
a couple approaches,
bare fingers twined
like the linked chains of a fence,
their shoulders as close as snow
packed by the county plow.

Slender boy and slender girl,
their faces radiant,
they pass beneath pines
whose branches are burdened
by the chilled innocence
of the fallen snow.

COLORADO PLATEAU

He taught them a poem
is not Folgers Instant Coffee
but layered lime that loves
the sandy ledge beneath it
stone on stone.

Its body reclines in geologic folds
and you must look and look
before it springs to life
as an Indian paintbrush
adorned with its sepaled
flame of meaning.

MIDWINTER WORDS

Lowland cottonwoods
lean leafless
over Oak Creek.
Robins bundle
on their clenched branches
as juncos probe
the shriveled grasses.

When dark descends
a pale race
lays fires
on hill and heath.
A triumph of light
confronts the fading sun.

Snow falls windless
and the season
is clothed.

FAR BEYOND FALL

Capuchin peaks lift hooded heads,
snow under foot.

Behind us the woods are forever
and we walk on
seeking the natural art
of a nature that is god
and a god that is nature,
small things our joined hands can hold.

When we return it is night,
stars rustle and whisper.

THE VOICES OF MARSHALL LAKE

Riding winter rushes,
yellow-headed blackbirds
release subdued whistles
from a haven of evening solitude
on this wholly natural lake.

I approach the resurrected frogs
whose shrill and saw-toothed song
speaks to the rising night;
the sullen voice of an American bittern
primes its pump and hammers its stake
into the heart of a bog,
a haunted sound.

Savoring their companionship,
redheads in staggered flight,
the male a wing beat behind,
arch their wings to splash down
in the south-end shallows.

Leaning against furrows
of orange-encrusted bark,
I watch through the leafless branches
of my outpost oak
a flock of blackbirds
rise from the island marsh,
swirl like smoke in the sunset sky,

and mass above my head
in the top of a shattered pine.

They chatter and scold
in the gathering dusk;
a sudden hush,
then the flock bursts out
from the pine's bare limbs
taking back their loaned lives
in a crescendo of wings
like breaking surf.

I grow old waiting like this oak,
learn patience from malpaís
and a moon that drops its fire
upon the restless lake.

When a planet appears in the south
only the frogs are strident,
marsh birds and waterfowl bedded down
in the wind-chilled hands of night.

TREASURES OF EARTH

Hoof prints deep in the dust
along the path to the forest gate
show that there are elk
flowing through our woods
with all the grace of water.

They track between the willow and the oak
back into the boundless pines
a moving darkness
in the shadowed distance
of the woods.

IN THE PENULTIMATE DARK

In the penultimate dark
the White Horse Hills
wait for these lines
to turn to light.

Rheingold flares
through the cloud's steep pass
till copper melts
to labile tears
in the heart's crucible.

Storm light falls back
upon the high villages to the north
while the raw coinage of the season
litters the cart path to Michael's Brook
and four hawks ride the flow
of Fern Mountain.

Prostrate on this prairie ridge
I render unto October
my privileged life
with all its truths and frailties;
bole dust of aspen
clings to my lips
like broken chalk.

Blasted pines
in least light burnt by death
front the pliant greenery
of these autumn groves.

The wind-soft silence
of this hill
lies in frost-naked gullies
too deep for the knife of feeling.

Figures in feathered costumes
stream down to thicket earth
to the pale shrubbery of fern and aspen;
coasting on light and shadow
two hawks plummet together
their pale underbodies
seen for a touching moment.

As late lupines spread welcoming fingers
below grass blond at the tips,
my foot falls into the swollen soil.

DRY LAKE ELEGY

Waist high in summer grasses
one returns and does not return
before the high clear days of September
fade the lake-bed meadows.

A daughter kneels
at graves where dogs
forever roam off leash
through aspen, fir, and pine.

After the season of rains
most of what we see
lives as we do now
in the mold of ancient trees.

We climb past fallen firs
and frost-split stones
to the wooded ridge
above a wildflower sea.

Below us lies Dry Lake Tank
where salamanders die
from an unknown chemistry
to become food for aquatic beetles.

Passionate in the black anger
of their hunger,

the vibrating masses of life and death
drift slowly ashore.

No one cries up the plague's dire toll;
we only know that the salamanders are dying,
the vernal lake gone to meadow,
all a strangeness, a mystery, a longing.

If I were to sit for an hour on this rock,
for an hour overlooking this dry lake bed,
this wheel-rutted, frog-slimed,
sea of compositae,

I might learn
that the skies cloud, the skies clear;
that the snows fall, the snows melt,
and the cycle of rain will see us again.

But there is no time;
ground water gathers
where redwings whistle
and all is a strangeness, a mystery, a longing.

A FEW AFTERWORDS:
ON THE PRACTICE OF POETRY

GOAL: The goal of a poet is to create a pattern of lines containing sounds and images that, in the fewest possible words, allows the individual who reads or hears them to experience a genuine emotion.

LINES: Lines can be of equal length or of varying length. A suggested practice is to use "spoken phrase length lines" determined by the natural pauses made in speaking.

METER OR BEAT: Meter involves the use of the natural pattern of stressed syllables in a spoken word to create a beat. The meter that dominates all poems written in English is iambic, with variations, and is that of the human heart: "thump/THUMP, thump/THUMP"; that is, an unstressed syllable followed by a stressed syllable. Lines usually contain at least two beats but no more than five. They are often grouped into stanzas, as in Emily Dickenson's poem, which has four and three beats alternating.

> "Farther in summer than the birds
> Pathetic from the grass
> A minor nation celebrates
> Its unobtrusive mass."

— Emily Dickenson "Farther in summer than the birds"

Sometimes the basis for the stanza is grammatical; that is, a single sentence. Other times it is formal or highly patterned, e.g., Shakespeare's Sonnets. One convention that has distinguished poetry from prose is that each line begins with a capital letter. However, free verse poems often do not follow it, and the use of capitals and other punctuation may follow the same rules of prose.

RHYME: Regular patterns of rhymes are not followed in free verse—that's why it's called "free"—but rhymes are often used, and these rhymes can be positioned not only at the ends of lines, but in the middle or at the beginning of the line.

Perfect rhyme (also known as exact, full, or true rhyme) requires the stressed vowel sound to be identical, such as hark, stark, and lark.

Imperfect rhyme (also called partial, slanted, half, near, sprung, off, lazy, oblique or approximate rhyme) has stressed sound that is similar, but not identical, such as "bear/beer"; "hop/hope"; "late/make".

SOUND: Assonance is the repetition in one or more lines of a similar vowel sound. Consonance is the repetition of a similar consonant. (E.g., a perfect rhyme contains both assonance and consonance). Alliteration is consonance at the beginning of a word. A good example of a free verse use of rhyme is this:
"The sunlight on the garden
Hardens and grows cold."
— *Louis MacNeice "The Sunlight on the Garden"*

DICTION: Words in English with Germanic roots from an Anglo-Saxon linguistic origin are largely of one or two syllables and generate more emotion than words that entered English after the Norman French Invasion of England in 1066 A.D.. These "Latinate" words tend to have more syllables and are more abstract, pretentious, and less "down to earth". Hence, say, "horse" not "equine"; "hate" not "antipathy", etc..

IMAGES: An image is a word that creates a specific picture in the mind of the reader or listener. Poems that are highly

160

visual generate strong feeling. Poems that are vague, abstract, or general in their choice of words have less emotional power.

A few examples…

Most vivid:
> "The big fish tubs are completely lined
> with layers of beautiful herring scales
> and the wheelbarrows are similarly plastered
> with creamy iridescent coats of mail,
> with small iridescent flies crawling on them."

— Elizabeth Bishop "At the Fishhouses"

Less vivid:
> "The fish tubs are covered with scales,
> and the wheelbarrows are crawling with flies."

Least vivid:
> "The fish tubs and wheelbarrows are filthy."

A FINAL WORD: To learn poetry, listen to poetry. Read widely and read out loud. Every evening before bed, read at least one great poem, hearing it in your mind's ear, and then reread it to notice how many of the devices here it contains.

If you haven't already, you will develop an ear for poetic language and imagery and acquire a sense of "what sounds good," which is all that's needed if the poet preserves his or her childhood sense of wonder and ability to "see" and "feel" the grandeur and mystery of the world that surrounds us.

In free writing and in the act of composing a poem, forget all about the devices mentioned above, all about technique. Trust in your sense of poetry as cultivated by reading. After the poem is finished to your satisfaction, read it to see what devices you have used unconsciously.

As your skill as a poet grows, your ability to explore life in all its complexity through poetry will grow until you may wish to try your hand at writing longer poems—narrative, meditative, speculative—that are centered on ideas conveyed through imagery, ideas that in turn evoke emotions. An example would be Rilke's Duino Elegies, which capture so magnificently the mission of a poet:

> "Praise this world to the angel,
>   not the unsayable one,
>   you won't impress him with your glorious
>   emotions; out there,
>   where he feels with more feeling,
>   you're but a novice.
>   Rather show him some common thing, shaped
>   through the generations,
>   that lives as ours,
>   near to our hand and in our sight."
> —*Rainer Maria Rilke "Duino Elegies: The Ninth Elegy"*

With best wishes for the proliferation and success of your own poems—

Judson D. McGehee

About the Author

Judson D. McGehee is an emeritus professor of English. Born in Akron, Ohio, he lived the nomadic life of an army child and experienced a diversity of environments, from the humid Panama Canal Zone at Fort Davis to the arid Arizona desert of Fort Huachuca.

After a tour of duty in the U.S. Army, he received a B.A. in Creative Writing and an M.A. in American Literature at Stanford University. A two-year fellowship took him to the University of Michigan, where he completed his Ph.D. in English.

During a thirty-year career at Northern Arizona University, he taught English and Creative Writing and served as advisor for the university's literary magazine *Pine Knots*. From 1976 to 1987, he wrote a weekly column "Northland Nature" for the *Arizona Daily Sun*.

He resides in Flagstaff, Arizona at the edge of the Coconino National Forest. For the latest on his publications, visit www.judsonmcgehee.com.

www.ingramcontent.com/pod-product-compliance
Lightning Source LLC
Chambersburg PA
CBHW022211050726
47590CB00002B/750